Favorite Chili Recipes

grilled steak chili

4 tablespoons minced garlic

¼ cup corn oil

3 cups chopped onion

1 can (14½ ounces) beef broth

3 cans (14½ ounces each) Mexican-style diced tomatoes
    with chilies, undrained

2 cans (14½ ounces each) crushed tomatoes

¼ cup plus 2 tablespoons chili powder

2 teaspoons ground cumin

2 teaspoons dried oregano leaves

1 teaspoon ground black pepper

4 pounds beef steak (preferably ribeye)

¼ cup masa harina (corn flour) or yellow cornmeal (optional)

    Minced cilantro, sliced green onions and sliced ripe olives
    for garnish

1. Place garlic and oil in large stock pot over low heat. Add onion;
cook and stir 5 minutes. Stir in beef broth, tomatoes, chili powder,
cumin, oregano and pepper; bring to a boil. Stir and reduce heat;
cover and simmer 1 to 2 hours or until thick.

2. Preheat electric grill or broiler. Grill steak until just browned on
both sides, about 8 minutes. Let rest 15 minutes. Slice into 2×½-inch
strips, reserving juices. Stir sliced steak and reserved juices into
chili; heat 5 to 10 minutes. If a thicker chili is desired, slowly sprinkle
in masa harina or corn meal; cook and stir 12 to 15 minutes or
until thickened. Garnish with cilantro, onions and olives.

Makes 10 to 12 servings

country sausage chili

2 pounds bulk spicy beef sausage
2 green bell peppers, seeded and chopped
2 cups chopped onion
1 tablespoon chopped garlic
2 cans (28 ounces each) crushed tomatoes
2 cans (4 ounces each) diced green chilies, drained
¼ cup ground chili powder
¼ cup molasses
1 tablespoon brown mustard seeds
2 teaspoons red pepper flakes
1 bay leaf
   Hot pepper sauce to taste

1. Brown beef sausage in large Dutch oven over medium heat. Drain fat, leaving 2 tablespoons fat in pot with browned sausage. Break sausage into chunks. Stir in bell peppers, onion and garlic. Cook and stir about 5 to 8 minutes or until onion is translucent.

2. Add crushed tomatoes, diced green chilies, chili powder, molasses, mustard seeds, red pepper flakes, bay leaf and hot sauce. Simmer about 1 hour or until thickened. Remove and discard bay leaf. Serve with biscuits or cornbread, if desired.

Makes 6 to 8 servings

red & green no-bean chili

4 pounds ground beef chuck (preferably large grind)
¼ cup chili powder, or to taste
2 tablespoons minced garlic
3 banana peppers, seeded and sliced
2 large onions, chopped
1 can (28 ounces) diced tomatoes with green chilies, undrained
1 can (14½ ounces) beef broth
2 cans (4 ounces each) diced green chilies, drained
2 tablespoons ground cumin
2 tablespoons ground hot paprika
2 tablespoons malt or cider vinegar
1 tablespoon dried oregano leaves
   Hot pepper sauce to taste
   Diced avocado and red onions for garnish

1. Brown beef in large Dutch oven over medium heat. Drain excess fat. Add chili powder, garlic, sliced peppers and chopped onions. Reduce heat to medium-low and cook and stir 30 minutes.

2. Add tomatoes, beef broth, green chilies, cumin, paprika, vinegar, oregano and hot pepper sauce. Cook 30 minutes, stirring occasionally. Garnish with diced avocado and red onions.

Makes 8 servings

red & green no-bean chili

beef chuck chili

½ cup olive oil
5 pounds beef chuck roast, trimmed of fat
3 cups minced onions
4 poblano chilies, seeded and diced*
2 serrano chilies, seeded and diced*
2 tablespoons minced garlic
2 green bell peppers, seeded and diced
3 jalapeño peppers, seeded and diced**
1 can (28 ounces) crushed tomatoes
1 tablespoon ground cumin
¼ cup hot pepper sauce
   Black pepper to taste
4 ounces Mexican lager beer (optional)

If fresh chilies are unavailable, use 2 cans (14 ounces each) Mexican green chilies and add dried ground chili powder for more heat.

**Jalapeño peppers can sting and irritate the skin. Wear rubber gloves when handling peppers and do not touch your eyes. Wash hands after handling.*

Slow Cooker Directions

1. Heat olive oil in large skillet over medium-high heat until hot. Add chuck roast. Sear on both sides. Remove beef to slow cooker.

2. Place onions, chilies and garlic in skillet. Reduce heat to low. Cook and stir 7 minutes. Add to slow cooker. Add crushed tomatoes. Cover; cook on LOW 4 to 5 hours or until beef is fork-tender.

3. Shred beef. Stir in cumin, hot pepper sauce, pepper and beer, if desired. Serve mixture over rice or cornbread.

Makes 8 to 10 servings

beef chuck chili

triathlete's turkey chili

2 tablespoons vegetable oil
2 medium onions, finely chopped
2 small red or green bell peppers, finely chopped
2 pounds 95% lean ground turkey
2 cans (14½ ounces each) diced tomatoes
1 can (14½ ounces) beef broth
1 cup water
¼ cup tomato paste
2 teaspoons chili powder
  Salt and black pepper to taste
1 can (15 ounces) kidney beans, rinsed and drained
1 can (15 ounces) pinto beans, rinsed and drained
  Cooked rice or cornbread
  Sour cream, shredded Cheddar cheese and green onion
    slices for garnish (optional)

1. Heat oil in Dutch oven. Add onions and peppers; cook and stir 3 minutes over medium heat. Add turkey; cook 3 minutes, stirring to break up meat. Stir in tomatoes, broth, water, tomato paste, chili powder, salt and pepper. Bring to a boil. Reduce heat and simmer 30 minutes, stirring often. If chili is too thick, add water, ½ cup at a time, until desired consistency is reached.

2. Add beans and cook 10 minutes or until beans are hot. Serve with rice or cornbread. Garnish with sour cream, cheese and green onion, if desired.   *Makes 8 servings*

Prep Time: 30 minutes
Cook Time: 40 minutes

triathlete's turkey chili

california turkey chili

1¼ cups chopped onion
1 cup chopped green bell pepper
2 cloves garlic, minced
3 tablespoons vegetable oil
1 can (28 ounces) kidney beans, drained
1 can (28 ounces) stewed tomatoes, undrained
1 cup red wine or water
3 cups cubed cooked California-grown turkey
1 tablespoon chili powder
1 tablespoon chopped fresh cilantro *or* 1 teaspoon dried coriander
1 teaspoon crushed red pepper
½ teaspoon salt
   Shredded Cheddar cheese (optional)
   Additional chopped onion (optional)
   Additional chopped fresh cilantro (optional)

Cook and stir onion, green pepper, garlic and oil in large saucepan over high heat until tender. Add beans, tomatoes with liquid, wine, turkey, chili powder, cilantro, red pepper and salt. Cover; simmer 25 minutes or until heated through. Top with cheese, onion or cilantro, if desired.   *Makes 6 servings*

*Favorite recipe from **California Poultry Federation***

cincinnati 5-way chili

¾ pound ground turkey
1 cup chopped onion, divided
3 cloves garlic, minced
1 can (8 ounces) reduced-sodium tomato sauce
¾ cup water
1 to 2 tablespoons chili powder
1 tablespoon unsweetened cocoa powder
1 to 2 teaspoons cider vinegar
1 teaspoon ground cinnamon
½ teaspoon ground allspice
½ teaspoon ground paprika
1 bay leaf
⅛ teaspoon ground cloves (optional)
   Salt and black pepper
8 ounces hot cooked spaghetti
½ cup (2 ounces) shredded fat-free Cheddar cheese
½ cup red kidney beans, rinsed and drained

1. Cook and stir turkey in medium saucepan over medium heat about 5 minutes or until browned and no longer pink. Drain fat and discard. Add ½ cup onion and garlic; cook about 5 minutes or until onion is tender.

2. Add tomato sauce, water, chili powder, cocoa, vinegar, cinnamon, allspice, paprika, bay leaf and cloves, if desired; bring to a boil. Reduce heat and simmer, covered, 15 minutes, stirring occasionally. If thicker consistency is desired, simmer, uncovered, about 5 minutes more. Discard bay leaf; season to taste with salt and pepper.

3. Spoon spaghetti into bowls; spoon sauce over top and sprinkle with remaining ½ cup onion, cheese and beans.

Makes 4 servings

southwest bean chili

1 cup uncooked dried garbanzo beans
¾ cup uncooked dried red kidney beans
¾ cup uncooked dried black beans
5½ cups canned fat-free reduced-sodium chicken broth
4 cloves garlic, minced
3 ears fresh corn, shucked and kernels cut from cobs
2 medium green bell peppers, seeded and chopped
1 can (16 ounces) tomato sauce
1 can (14½ ounces) Mexican-style stewed tomatoes, undrained
3 tablespoons chili powder
1 tablespoon unsweetened cocoa powder
1 teaspoon ground cumin
½ teaspoon salt
4 cups hot cooked rice
Shredded cheese, ripe olive, avocado and green onion slices (optional)

1. Rinse beans thoroughly in colander under cold running water, picking out debris and any blemished beans.

2. Place beans in large bowl; cover with 4 inches of water. Let stand at room temperature overnight.

3. Drain beans. Combine with chicken broth and garlic in large heavy saucepan. Bring to a boil over high heat. Reduce heat to low; simmer, covered, 1 hour.

4. Add corn, bell peppers, tomato sauce, tomatoes with juice, chili powder, cocoa powder, cumin and salt to bean mixture. Cover partially; simmer 45 minutes or until beans are tender and mixture is thick.

5. Spoon rice into bowls; top with chili. Serve with cheese, olives, avocado and onions, if desired. *Makes 8 to 10 servings*

southwest bean chili

chili mole

1 pound ground beef
1 Spanish onion, diced
1 green bell pepper, seeded and diced
1 banana pepper, finely chopped
2 jalapeño peppers, finely chopped*
2 cloves garlic, finely chopped
2 cans (14½ ounces each) diced tomatoes
2 cans (15 ounces each) kidney beans, rinsed and drained
1 can (4 ounces) tomato paste
1 packet (2 ounces) Cincinnati-style chili seasoning
3 tablespoons unsweetened cocoa powder
2 tablespoons chili powder
1 tablespoon brown sugar
1 tablespoon lime juice

*Jalapeño peppers can sting and irritate the skin. Wear rubber gloves when handling peppers and do not touch your eyes. Wash hands after handling.

1. Brown ground beef in large Dutch oven over medium heat. Cook until no longer pink. Drain fat and discard.

2. Add onion and bell pepper. Cook and stir until onion is translucent.

3. Add banana pepper, jalapeño peppers and garlic; cook and stir 3 minutes.

4. Add tomatoes and beans.

5. Stir in tomato paste, chili seasoning, cocoa, chili powder, brown sugar and lime juice. Cover and simmer 1 hour.

Makes 6 servings

chili mole

chili verde

½ to ¾ pound boneless lean pork, cut into 1-inch cubes
1 large onion, halved and thinly sliced
6 cloves garlic, chopped or sliced
½ cup water
1 pound fresh tomatillos
1 can (14½ ounces) chicken broth
1 can (4 ounces) diced mild green chilies, drained
1 teaspoon ground cumin
1½ cups cooked navy or Great Northern beans *or* 1 can
    (15 ounces) Great Northern beans, rinsed and drained
½ cup lightly packed fresh cilantro, chopped
    Jalapeño peppers,* sliced (optional)

Jalapeño peppers can sting and irritate the skin. Wear rubber gloves when handling peppers and do not touch your eyes. Wash hands after handling.

1. Place pork, onion, garlic and water in large saucepan. Cover; simmer over medium-low heat 30 minutes, stirring occasionally (add more water if necessary). Uncover; boil over medium-high heat until liquid evaporates and meat browns.

2. Stir in tomatillos and broth. Cover; simmer over medium heat 20 minutes or until tomatillos are tender. Pull tomatillos apart with 2 forks. Add chilies and cumin.

3. Cover; simmer over medium-low heat 45 minutes or until meat is tender and pulls apart easily. (Add more water or broth, if necessary, to keep liquid at same level.) Add beans; simmer 10 minutes or until heated through. Stir in cilantro. Top with jalapeño peppers, if desired.   *Makes 4 servings*

vegetarian chili

1 tablespoon vegetable oil
1 cup finely chopped onion
1 cup chopped red bell pepper
2 tablespoons minced jalapeño pepper*
1 clove garlic, minced
1 can (28 ounces) crushed tomatoes
1 can (15 ounces) black beans, rinsed and drained
1 can (15 ounces) garbanzo beans, rinsed and drained
½ cup corn
¼ cup tomato paste
1 teaspoon sugar
1 teaspoon ground cumin
1 teaspoon dried basil leaves
1 teaspoon chili powder
¼ teaspoon black pepper
  Sour cream and shredded Cheddar cheese (optional)

Jalapeño peppers can sting and irritate the skin. Wear rubber gloves when handling peppers and do not touch your eyes. Wash hands after handling.

Slow Cooker Directions

1. Heat oil in large nonstick skillet over medium-high heat until hot. Add onion, bell pepper, jalapeño pepper and garlic; cook and stir 5 minutes or until vegetables are tender.

2. Transfer vegetables to slow cooker. Add remaining ingredients except sour cream and cheese; mix well. Cover; cook on LOW 4 to 5 hours. Garnish with sour cream and cheese, if desired.

Makes 4 servings

vegetarian chili

baked black bean chili

1½ pounds 90% lean ground beef
¼ cup chopped sweet onion
¼ cup chopped green bell pepper
1 can (15 ounces) black beans, rinsed and drained
1 can (14½ ounces) diced tomatoes with green chilies
1 can (14½ ounces) beef broth
1 can (8 ounces) tomato sauce
5 tablespoons chili powder
1 tablespoon sugar
1 tablespoon ground cumin
1 teaspoon dried minced onion
⅛ teaspoon garlic powder
⅛ teaspoon ground ginger
2 cups (8 ounces) shredded Mexican cheese blend

1. Preheat oven to 350°F. Cook and stir beef, onion and bell pepper in large skillet over medium-high heat until meat is no longer pink. Drain and transfer to 4-quart casserole.

2. Add remaining ingredients except cheese; stir until well blended. Cover and bake 30 minutes, stirring every 10 minutes. Uncover; top with cheese. Return to oven about 5 minutes or until cheese melts.   *Makes 6 to 8 servings*

baked black bean chili

spicy quick and easy chili

1 pound ground beef

1 large clove garlic, minced

1 can (15¼ ounces) DEL MONTE® Whole Kernel Golden
     Sweet Corn, drained

1 can (16 ounces) kidney beans, drained

1½ cups salsa, mild, medium or hot

1 can (4 ounces) diced green chiles, undrained

1. Brown meat with garlic in large saucepan; drain.

2. Add remaining ingredients. Simmer, uncovered, 10 minutes,
stirring occasionally. Sprinkle with chopped green onions, if
desired.   *Makes 4 servings*

Prep and Cook Time: 15 minutes